Getting a Job in Social Work

Getting a Job in Social Work

Dona J. Young

Indiana University Northwest

Bassim Hamadeh, CEO and Publisher
Amy Smith, Associate Editorial Manager
Abbey Hastings, Senior Production Editor
Jess Estrella, Senior Graphic Designer
Kylie Bartolome, Licensing Specialist
Natalie Piccotti, Director of Marketing
Kassie Graves, Senior Vice President, Editorial
Alia Bales, Director, Project Editorial and Production

Printed in the United States of America.

Brief Contents

Contents

Introduction

There is no passion to be found playing small, in settling for a life that is less than the one you are capable of living.

—Nelson Mandela

Regardless of your achievements, looking for a job can make you question everything you have ever achieved. That is because the job-search process is different from other activities and projects. You are not just using your talents to solve a problem—you have become the *central theme* of the project. Finding a job is a full-time job, and whether you like it or not, *you* are the focal point—the job itself is secondary.

Right now, you may feel more confident using your skills than talking about them. Verbalizing your job survival skills equates to marketing yourself; to do that, you first need to identify your unique qualities so that you can prepare your résumé and ready yourself for interviewing. This book walks you through a process to define your unique *career profile*, which includes identifying your skills and qualities that set you apart from the crowd.

In the process, you will develop your *career portfolio*. Some of the documents you will prepare include your résumé, of course, but also a cover letter, a thank-you letter, and a business card. Then, you will be ready to review interview questions. After you have prepared for your job search, you will be prepared to use websites, such as SocialWorkers.org and CareerBuilder.com, among others. As you complete your portfolio, you may also feel motivated to network in local or national social work organizations, on site or online. *Networking is still the most effective job-search tool.*

To prepare you for your job search and beyond, this book is broken into the following parts:

- Part 1: Preparing for Your Job Search
- Part 2: Job-Search Letters and Résumés
- Part 3: The Interview
- Part 4: Leadership, Core Values, and Purpose
- Quick Guide to Email and Letter Formatting

When you have completed this book, you will be able to the following:

- Identify your unique career profile, specifying transferable skills and experience.
- Develop a career portfolio that includes a hard-copy résumé, e-résumé, and business card.
- Compose a cover letter and a thank-you message.
- Develop a strategy to engage in networking opportunities, online and on site.
- Prepare for a traditional interview and behavioral interview.
- Identify your unique leadership skills, core values, and purpose.

You have worked hard to build your skills. Though searching for a job might feel daunting, the best response is to take action and stay active until you achieve your dreams. Do the work, and you will see the results.

Just remember, you can do anything you set your mind to, but it takes action, perseverance, and facing your fears.

—Gillian Anderson (1999)

PART 1

Preparing for Your Job Search

To get started on your job-search quest, you will first examine your unique skill set so that you are ready to prepare your résumé when the time comes. Before getting started on identifying your skills and abilities, let's examine the value of networking.

Networking

The best way to find a job is through networking. According to Matt Youngquist, president of Career Horizons,

> At least 70 percent, if not 80 percent, of jobs are not published, yet most people ... are spending 70 or 80 percent of their time surfing the net versus getting out there, talking to employers, taking some chances [and] realizing that the vast [majority] of hiring is friends and acquaintances hiring other trusted friends and acquaintances. (2017, as cited in Belli, 2017)

For example, you may have a better chance of getting an interview by contacting someone you know at a company than by contacting the human resources department. According to Ilana Gershon, "what [hiring managers] value most is a strong recommendation from someone who actually knows the applicant as a worker and can assure them that the person will be a good hire" (2017).

Build your network now. Professional networking groups give you a steady stream of new contacts. By doing an online search of groups that target your interests, you will find opportunities to use your social skills as you build your reputation and credibility. The following strategies can help you build a professional network:

- *Connect with people who have similar goals and values.* Stay active and involved on site and online.
- *Build your network before you need it.* Start now and network on an ongoing basis so that you make contacts, remain visible, and get the support you need.
- *View networking as a communication exchange, not a one-sided dialog.* Before you call on someone to network, articulate why the meeting would be *mutually* beneficial. Look for common interests, experiences, or shared acquaintances.
- *Reciprocate favors.* When you ask people for help, also ask what you can do for them in return. You may find that an opportunity that did not work out for you is perfect for someone else.
- *View organizations within your field as career opportunities.* Through professional organizations, you will meet new people and have experiences that enhance your leadership skills.
- *Continue to network within your organization.* By networking within your organization, you build relationships as you promote your visibility and flexibility.

Volunteer to serve on committees, participate in focus groups, and attend activities related to your interests. Find new friends by attending fundraising events for not-for-profit organizations. Treat everyone with respect, including support staff, such as mailroom and cleaning personnel.

Career Portfolio

All job seekers need to be organized and ready to present their credentials so that employers recognize their skills *at a glance*; the first screening of an applicant lasts only seconds, and employers seek to eliminate applicants at the beginning of the process. Something that sounds small, such as using an incorrect salutation in your cover letter, can be reason enough for some to toss out your letter and résumé.

Your first position is only the first step in your career, and you may find that you need to continue to reinvent yourself throughout your career. If you keep your mindset geared toward change, you will succeed.

Though you may never share your entire career portfolio with a prospective employer, preparing it will give you confidence and prepare you for even the unexpected during your job-search process. Here are some suggestions about what to include in your portfolio:

- *purpose statement*—To gain clarity and make effective career choices, write a purpose statement that reflects your life's mission.
- *résumé*—Prepare your traditional and electronic résumés, tailoring your résumé for each job. Keep your résumé to *a maximum* of two pages. For international organizations as well as for some academic and research positions, prepare a curriculum vitae.
- *work samples*—Select a few exhibits of your best work from previous jobs or classes: a letter, a report, a paper, and so on.
- *reference letters*—If you ask for letters up front, before you need them, you can use the salutation "Dear Hiring Manager" or "Dear Job-Search Committee." However, for specific positions, ask your reference to use the name of the person requesting the letter.
- *networking contacts*—Become an expert at networking on site and online. Once again, networking is still the best way to find a job, including e-networking on sites such as LinkedIn.
- *business card*—Design your own job-search card with your name, email address, phone number, and vital points about your skills.

While you will keep an electronic file of your documents so that your e-portfolio is readily available, also consider using a three-ring binder or folder to organize hard copies, just in case you need it. Here are a few other details on which you may want to take action:

- If you have a Facebook page, now is the time to edit it. Prospective employers routinely screen applicants' social networking activity and photos.
- If you do not have a professional-sounding email address, create one now. Use some form of your name, if possible, such as "myname@email.com."
- If you use other types of social media or post online at blogs, know that your electronic footprint follows you for a long time and may *never* go away.

The most important part of your job search is being able to verbalize your skills, qualities, and experience, so keep that in mind as you work through the remainder of this chapter.

Jobs in Social Work

The Occupational Outlook Handbook lists the following categories of social work positions:

- ***Child and family social workers*** protect vulnerable children and help families in need of assistance. They help families find housing or services, such as childcare, or apply for benefits, such as food stamps. They intervene when children are in danger of neglect or abuse. Some help arrange adoptions, locate foster families, or work to reunite families.
- ***School social workers*** work with teachers, parents, and school administrators to develop plans and strategies to improve students' academic performance and social development. They help students with problems such as aggressive behavior or bullying. Additionally, school social workers meet with families to discuss issues such as access to special education resources or frequent student absences.

- ***Healthcare social workers*** help clients understand their diagnosis and adjust their lifestyle, housing, or healthcare. For example, they may help people transition from the hospital to their homes and communities. In addition, they may provide information about services, such as home healthcare or support groups, to help clients manage their illness or disease. Social workers help doctors and other healthcare workers understand the effects that diseases and illnesses have on clients' mental and emotional health. Some healthcare social workers specialize in geriatric social work, hospice and palliative care, or medical social work.
- ***Mental health and substance abuse social workers*** help clients with mental illnesses or addictions. They provide information on services, such as support groups and 12-step programs, to help clients cope with their illness. These workers often are licensed clinical social workers. (U.S. Bureau of Labor Statistics, 2024)

Skills, Not Titles or Degrees

Do not limit yourself by being too attached to a job title, and keep your objective flexible; new job titles are created every day, as traditional titles are eliminated. Though a title will not follow you throughout your career, your skills, talents, and achievements will. Identify how your skills transfer to *any* business environment, and you will gain a broader understanding of what you offer.

Transferable Skills

Defining marketable skills is a challenge, especially when you think you do not have any. By defining what you have achieved, you are able to see the unique qualities that you bring to an employer. Some of your skills have come from interests or hobbies, and you may not even be aware of what you have learned. Start to develop your job search profile by exploring these basic areas:

- working with people
- identifying knowledge you can apply
- working on tasks
- identifying personal qualities

Working With People

How do you work with people? Consider formal and informal experiences at school, at your place of worship, with volunteer groups, on part- and full-time jobs, in sports activities, and in associations. Here are some terms to open up your thinking. As you go through the list, notice your impressions as well as specific experiences that come to mind:

Counseling
Giving Feedback
Receiving Feedback
Marketing
Expressing Humor
Listening Actively
Leading
Organizing Projects
Organizing Events
Delegating
Care Giving
Selling
Advising
Negotiating
Mediating
Entertaining
Serving
Phoning/Soliciting
Cleaning
Being Compassionate
Fixing
Training
Evaluating
Facilitating
Working on Teams
Supervising
Working Independently
Being Flexible
Building Rapport
Being Resilient

List three to five qualities: ______________________________

____

Identifying Knowledge You Can Apply

What are your areas of expertise? In addition to formal learning, consider hobbies and interests. Read through the following list, and circle three or more of the items that reflect your abilities:

Writing (composing, editing, revising) / Communication

Languages (speaking, writing, translating, interpreting) / Research / Social Policy / Group Practice

Global Communication / Communities and Societies / Business Management / Accounting / Psychology /

Sociology / Social Work / Counseling / Physical Sciences / Math / Statistics / Budgeting / Biology / Medicine

Pharmaceuticals / Music / Instruments / Child Care / Early Child Development

Elementary or Secondary Education / Voice / Theater / Film Making /Art / Archeology / Anthropology / Law

Criminal / Civil / Police Science / Political Science / History / Social Sciences / Sports / Nutrition / Cosmetology

Physical Therapy / Organizational Development / Human Resource Development / Fundraising

Graphic Arts or Design / Interior Design

List three to five abilities: ______________________________

____

Working on Tasks

What kinds of tasks can you perform? Consider all of the classes you have taken as well as job experience, paid or volunteer. Also consider your hobbies and interests; these activities are important to employers. Which tasks can you perform well? Which tasks do you enjoy? (Later in this chapter, you will list part- and full-time jobs.) Use the following list of nouns and verbs to generate a list of tasks you do well:

Work with Children / Counsel / Email / PowerPoint / Case Notes / Web Design

Manage / Solve Problems / Crisis Management / Analyze / Trouble Shoot / Survey

Care for Children and Elderly / Design / Paint / Draw / Sketch / Sculpt / Construct

Gather Information / Organize and File / Spreadsheets / Tables / Graphs / Letters

Behavior Management Plans / Agendas / Minutes / Reports / Proposals / Set Goals

Meet Quotas / Read / Write / Edit / Coach / Supervise / Anger Management /

Greet and Receive / Clean Houses or Offices / Play Music / Compose / Style Hair /

Drive / Word / Excel / WordPerfect / Harvard Graphics / Calendar Creator Plus

List three to five tasks you perform well: ______________________

____

Identifying Personal Qualities

You are unique whether you realize it or not. Close your eyes and reflect for a moment: What adjectives come to mind when you think of yourself? What are your personal qualities that shape you into who you are? Select three or more of the following qualities that describe you:

reliable
dependable
motivated
self-starter
persistent
optimistic
self-reliant
strong
independent
capable
fast learner
supportive
eager
task-oriented
purposeful
focused
disciplined
friendly
persuasive
artistic
committed
easy-going
encouraging
flexible
confident
decisive
enthusiastic
creative
balanced
open minded
accepting
prompt
courteous
patient
dedicated
supportive
loyal
adaptable
compassionate
ethical
competent
kind
helpful
determined
honest
responsible
self-learner
passionate
resilient
practical
tenacious
energetic

List three to five personal qualities: ______________________________

____

Stating Growing Edges Positively

Now that you have established several good qualities, list an area or two that you wish to improve; call them your *growing edges* if you wish. Prospective employers do not expect you to be perfect, and they will ask about your weaknesses. By responding effectively, you have the perfect opportunity to show that your self-awareness leads to self-growth.

Because they interview hundreds of applicants, human resource professionals can see through insincere answers. By being honest yet optimistic about your weaknesses, you will actually score points. State your weakness in a constructive way:

Do Not Say: I'm late getting my work done sometimes, and I need to get control of my schedule.

Do Say: Sometimes, I get so involved in solving a problem that I lose track of time. I'm working on time management so that my schedule is more balanced. Overall, it feels as if I have more time and more control over my time.

Do Not Say: I feel frustrated working on a team, especially when others don't hold their weight. Sometimes, I'm very critical.

Do Say: I prefer working independently than working on a team because I have more control over a project, but I am becoming more patient as well as learning how to give constructive feedback to move a project along.

List one or two growing edges: ______________________________

____

How can you state your growing edge or weakness in a positive way?

____

____

Asking for Feedback

When you are on a job interview, one of the questions that you may be asked is, "How do others perceive you?" To prepare, ask three people who know you well to describe your skills and attitudes. Choose people who are positive and supportive. Let them know that you are doing research for your job-search profile. If they are willing, ask if you could receive your feedback in writing via a short note or email so that you are able to refer to it later.

Here are some questions you can ask:

- What are three adjectives you would use to describe me?
- What are some tasks you have seen me do well?
- In your eyes, what achievements have I made?
- Do you consider me a team player, a leader, a self-starter?
- What do you think are my growing edges or areas in which I can improve?

Take a few moments to reflect on the input you have received and record it, especially if it is all verbal. You may be surprised at how positively others perceive you. If you feel uncomfortable when you hear good things about yourself, simply say *thank you* and move on. The same advice is true if you hear negative things. Keep an open mind, and use the feedback to develop objectives for self-growth.

What do others say about you? What feedback have you received?

____

____

Summarizing Work Experience

Make a list of all paid or volunteer jobs you have had. For each, specify how long you had the job. Instead of giving start and end dates, list the months and years and then quantify the time, as in the following example:

Supportive care, part-time caregiver	January to March, 2023	7 weeks
	July to August, 2023	6 weeks
	December, 2023	3 weeks
	Total	about 4 months

Though you are concerned with dates, you also want to have an idea of the amount of time on the job. Quantify your experiences in terms of years and months or even weeks. After you tally the specifics, you can list your experience as follows:

Supportive Care, part-time caregiver

January to December, 2023	4 months

Now, take a moment to record the jobs you have held and tally your job experience in months and years.

Job 1: Title/Company	**Dates**	**Time**
____________________	____________________	________________
	____________________	________________

Job 2: Title/Company	**Dates**	**Time**
____________________	____________________	________________
	____________________	________________

Job 3: Title/Company	**Dates**	**Time**
____________________	____________________	________________
	____________________	________________

For each position, write a sentence or two that demonstrates the skills that you applied. Write active sentences using strong verbs, and avoid filler verbs and phrases, such as “I learned how to” or “I gained experience doing,” as shown in the examples that follow:

Weak: While working as a special education assistant at Educational Support, *I learned how to communicate* with learners who lacked confidence.

Revised: While working as a special education assistant at Educational Support, *I communicated* with learners who lacked confidence.

Weak: While I volunteered at Sojourner Truth House, *I gained experience from assisting some of the* staff distribute items from the food pantry.

Revised: While volunteering at Sojourner Truth House, *I assisted* staff distributing items from the food pantry.

Weak: As a coaching assistant at Boys and Girls YMCA, *I was able to learn how* to provide personal attention to each child.

Revised: As a coaching assistant at Boys and Girls YMCA, *I assisted each child based on their individual needs, giving feedback and encouragement to keep them motivated.*

When you go on an interview, be prepared with an example to demonstrate one of your achievements. For example, perhaps, you are the first person in your family to graduate from college or maybe you recently won an award. These types of notable experiences give prospective employers insight into your personality and interests as well as how you apply your skills.

Of course, use discretion in choosing which achievements to cite. A prospective employer does not want to hear about personal milestones, such as engagements or weddings, and no matter how cute your children are, save those stories for your friends and relatives.

Coaching Tip

Social Media Alert

Potential employers are not impressed by the same things your friends are impressed by, so "clean up" your social media sites *before* you start searching for your dream job. Also, be very selective about what you tweet or post online, as it may follow you throughout your career. Many hearts have by broken by a moment of indiscretion. Finally, if you don't have a professional-sounding email address for your résumé and other job-search documents, *get one now.*

Personal Business Cards

Especially if you are new to the job market, create a business card. Select a few accomplishments and list them as bullet points on your card:

Jane Addams 312.555.1212
ja@email.com

BSW, Rockford University

- Three years of experience as teaching assistant
- Compassionate, Creative, Focused, and Motivated
- Excellent GPA and References

Image 1.1

Your new business card is a useful tool for networking, providing your contact information and reminding associates of your skills.

Writing Workshop

A. Researching Careers in Social Work

Instructions: Research opportunities by doing an internet search. Go to a job-search website, such as careers.socialwork.org or careerbuilder.com, and ask yourself the following:

- What are some different types of positions that are available in social work?
- What positions are you interested in?
- What qualities, skills, and types of experience are organizations seeking?
- What are some goals you can set for yourself to become more marketable for your dream job?

B. Researching Social Work Organizations

Instructions: Identify social work organizations you can join:

- What are some social work organizations that you can join now while you are a student?
- What are some organizations you can join in the future as a professional?
- What are some other benefits of joining a professional social work organization?

Research your community, and perform an online search for professional organizations that can offer you the benefit of gaining experience and networking. Write a short summary of your findings, and share it with a colleague; compare notes. What did you learn from each other?

C. The Social Worker Interview

Instructions: Identify a social worker who would be willing to give you a brief interview about their job, and ask them the following:

1. What is your position, and how long have you held it?
2. What was your motivation for going into the field of social work?
3. What are some of the most challenging aspects of your job? What are the most satisfying?
4. What advice would you give a novice going into the field of social work?
5. Do you have any job-search tips for entering the field of social work?

After your interview, write a summary, formatting it in APA style, according to your instructor's instructions.

PART 2

Job-Search Letters and Résumés

You are now ready to prepare your most important job-search documents, which will give you confidence and set you apart from the crowd of other job seekers.

Job-Search Letters

Letters are important tools for initiating, developing, and following up with contacts and job prospects. Even though email seems to be used for just about everything nowadays, a hard-copy letter still makes a strong impression. Two types of letters crucial to the job-search process include cover letters and thank-you letters. Tailor every letter that you write to the specific position you are going after and the organization to which you are sending it. In addition, some prospective employers prefer that all application letters and résumés be submitted online, while others prefer to receive hard copies. Check each organization's preference as you engage in your job search. Next, you will review how to customize your letter.

Cover Letters

Send a cover letter with your résumé, or send a cover message, if you send your résumé online. State why you would be the best person for the job, and highlight your accomplishments. While your letter—or message—may not get you the job, a poorly written one will keep you from getting in the door. Here are some guidelines that relate to job-search letters:

- *Know the name and title of the person to whom you are writing.* Do not address a letter to "Dear Sir" or "Dear Madam." Go to the company website or call to find out the addressee's name and its correct spelling. If you cannot find a name, use a salutation such as "Dear Hiring Manager" or "Dear Search Committee" (avoid using "To Whom It May Concern").
- *Find out whether the prospective employer prefers to receive résumés online or through the mail.* If you submit an application letter and résumé online, email it to yourself first and print out your file to make sure it looks professional.
- *Stress what you can offer the organization.* Rather than focus on what you are looking for in a position, stress how your skills can benefit the organization.
- *Develop a follow-up plan.* Take charge; do not expect others to contact you after they receive your information.
- *Aim for perfection.* Your written communication creates a strong impression. A letter of application presents high stakes. Write in active voice, use the *you* viewpoint, and be concise.

A strong cover letter has an opening to capture the reader's attention but also identifies the job for which you are applying.

Example: The opportunity listed with CareerBuilder for a direct care worker is a great fit with my background and qualifications; my résumé is attached.

Example: Our mutual colleague, Andy Garcia, suggested that I have the talent and qualifications you are looking for in a bilingual crisis counselor. My enclosed résumé highlights some of that experience.

In the next paragraph, explain your special skills by listing some of your major accomplishments or qualifications that are relevant to the position you are seeking.

Example: As a recent college graduate, I have experience in youth and family services. My degree in social work includes a three-month internship. As an intern, I supported three case managers who trusted me with clients and with managing their paperwork.

In the last part of your cover letter, request an interview. If you wish, state that you will call within a specific time frame to find a mutually agreeable time to meet. Note that even if you do not state that you will follow up, you still can.

Example: I'd appreciate the opportunity to meet with you to discuss how my background can benefit your agency. I will contact you the week of June 12 to see if we can meet.

Example: I'd appreciate the opportunity to meet with you and look forward to hearing from you.

Thus, the first paragraph identifies the job, the second paragraph explains your special skills, and the third paragraph provides the call to action. If you make a commitment to call, be sure to follow through. If the person is not available, ask if there is another time that would be convenient for you to call back. Leave your name and number, but do not feel slighted if you do not get a callback; the responsibility for communication is on your shoulders.

Rosalie D. Lindsey
1212 Arquilla Lane
Winter Haven, FL 33884
(863) 555-1212 | rdl@email.com

January 6, 2024

Ms. Jane Fleming
Department of Child Services
8007 Nashville Boulevard
Tallahassee, FL 35316

Dear Ms. Fleming:

Thank you for the time that you spent with me at the recent CSWE conference discussing opportunities at your agency.

I will receive my MSW from Best College this spring; my résumé is enclosed. As you can see, my part-time jobs would contribute to my success as a behavioral health technician. In addition to my volunteer work at Crisis Intervention Center, I have family members with special needs, giving me experience in advocating for the disabled.

I will follow up with you soon to find out if there is a convenient time for us to meet.

Sincerely,

Rosalie D. Lindsey
Résumé Enclosed

FIGURE 2.1 Sample Cover Letter

Writing Tip: Introductions

In writing, don't introduce yourself by name, as you would if you were meeting someone in person. Instead, start your letter with your purpose for writing. The reader will know who you are based on your typed signature:

Weak:	My name is Silvia Jones, and I am interested in applying for the position of childcare advocate.
Revised:	Your position for childcare advocate is a perfect match for my skills and experience.

Follow-Up Letters and Thank-You Notes

Two of the most powerful tools in your job-search toolkit are a follow-up email and a handwritten thank-you note. Your note encourages your new networking associate or potential employer to feel good about meeting with you or making calls on your behalf. By writing a formal thank-you letter, you have another opportunity to show your commitment and high standards. While your letter allows you to restate a major skill or accomplishment, focus on elevating the discussion by noting the special qualities of the organization and its people, removing the attention from yourself. Write a letter that is simple, friendly, and genuine. Customize each letter, email message, and handwritten note by specifically referring to something you discussed or observed during your interview. Get a business card from each of your contacts so that sending a note or email takes less effort. Surprisingly, no matter how good the results are from sending thank-you notes, few people actually send them.

Dear Elaine,

Thank you for sharing your valuable time and advice for my job search.

I have contacted John, as you suggested, and he was helpful in recommending me to contact an agency that has an opening for a case worker and family advocate. Both positions appeal to me. I will keep you informed on my progress; in the meantime, if I can support your work in any way, feel free to contact me.

Good luck with assisting your clients at the new community center.

All the best,

Sophie

FIGURE 2.2 Sample Thank-You Note for Networking

Writing Tip: Create a Letterhead

For your job-search documents, create a letterhead for yourself that contains your contact information:

- You can either center the information at the top of the page, block it at the left or right margin, or choose other creative styles. (See examples in this text.)
- By putting your letterhead in the header, you gain space as well as make your letterhead look more "official."
    - Simply go to the top of the page and double-click.
    - Once the header opens, type in or paste in your contact information.
- Once you create your letterhead, use it for all of your job-search documents, such as your cover letter, résumé, and thank-you letters.

Rosalie D. Lindsey
1212 Arquilla Lane
Winter Haven, FL 33884
(863) 555-1212 | rdl@email.com

May 5, 2024

Ms. Margaret Harris
Promising Care, Inc.
427 Arquilla Drive
Tampa, FL 33592

Dear Ms. Harris:

Thank you for interviewing me for the child welfare position.

Learning more about your agency reinforced my motivation to work in this field, and your agency's commitment to supporting children in need is reassuring and comforting. The professionalism that you and your staff displayed has reinforced my interest in this position.

If there is anything else you need from me, please let me know. I look forward to hearing from you soon.

Sincerely,

Rosalie D. Lindsey

FIGURE 2.3 Sample Thank-You Letter for Job Interview

Writing Tip: Templates

You will find an abundance of templates online to create your résumé and write your cover letter. While you might ultimately want to use a template, start with your "manually written" résumé first, which will give you more flexibility when you need to update it.

Also, keep your cover letter short and to the point. Don't feel inclined to cover too much information that is already listed on your résumé:

- The purpose of the cover letter is to encourage the recipient to review your résumé. (Remember to mention in your letter that you are enclosing your résumé, and then also include an enclosure notation.)
- The purpose of your résumé is to get an interview.

In writing, less is more. Shorter letters are more likely to be read than longer ones, and the same is true for messages.

The Résumé

Human resource executives and hiring managers receive hundreds of résumés for every job opening. Though you want your résumé to stand out, be careful about how you do it.

Brevity is critical. Highlight your experience effectively on one page; at any rate, do not exceed two pages. Also, *do not* use flamboyant fonts or fancy paper. Instead, use conservative fonts, such as Times New Roman and Arial. Use one style of font for the body and another for your letterhead and headings. For hard-copy résumés, use crisp, white, heavy-weight bond paper.

Chronological Formatting

The *chronological format* lists your education and work experience in order, starting with the most recent and working backward. This format is the most traditional, so readers find it easy to see a history of steady promotions or increased responsibility. Here are some tips:

- Create a letterhead that contains your contact information: name, address, phone, email address. *Note*: For a remote job, you don't need to include your address until you establish a relationship with your prospective employer.
- Use "Career Focus" or "Summary," rather than "Objective."
- Make sure prospective employers can identify the job or job category for which you are applying *at a glance*; tailor your résumé for each job you seek.
    - You can put the title of the job for which you are applying at the top of your résumé in place of or next to "Career Focus" or "Objective." (See the example provided in Figure 2.4.)
    - You can also create a "headline" that is 10 words or fewer. (See text box.)
- Be specific about accomplishments; quantify your achievements when possible.
- Apply parallel structure (represent words in a consistent form).
- Keep your résumé to one page if you can or two pages if you cannot.

- To gain space, you can leave off positions that are not relevant to the position for which you are applying; for less relevant positions, keep descriptions short.

On a traditional résumé, describe your work experience in verb phrases that begin with strong action verbs (e.g., present-tense verbs, such as "manage," "supervise," or "review," for current positions or past-tense verbs, such as "managed," "supervised," or "reviewed," for past positions). Write your résumé with the aim of answering questions *before* they arise. On your cover letter, fill in gaps of unemployment that might appear on your résumé. Employers assume you are telling the truth until they find out otherwise. When employers check specific details, they usually do so only after they have already decided to hire you.

Create a Headline

Under your letterhead, you can include a 10-word headline that captures the title of the job for which you are applying along with some of your important qualities, such as academic degrees and years of experience (Henderson, 2024):

BETTY J. KROCKER
Bloomington, IN 46368 | 219-555-5555 |
bjkrocker@email.com
Linkedin.com/in/bettyjkrocker

MSW GRADUATE STUDENT, 3.9 GPA, SEEKS INTERNSHIP IN CHILD ADVOCACY

ROSALIE D. LINDSEY

1212 Arquilla Lane
Winter Haven, FL 35319
(813) 555-1212 (H) • (813) 555-1212 (C)
pv@email.com

CAREER FOCUS: CHILD WELFARE SPECIALIST

Dedicated ***advocate for children with special needs*** with extensive experience as a caregiver at home and in nursing homes. Committed to assisting others; effective leader who can train and motivate.

SKILLS

Word, Excel, PowerPoint, WordPerfect, Lotus Notes, Calendar Creator Plus, Outlook (email), Internet (Orbitz and Expedia)

EXPERIENCE

Supportive Care, Tampa, Florida **June 2021 to Present**

Senior Care Assistant

- Assisting with bathing, grooming, and incontinence issues.
- Providing stabilization and assistance with walking.
- Preparing meals and cleaning up meal-related items.
- Providing medication reminders and appointment reminders.

EDUCATION

BSW, Best University, 2021
A.A., Communications, Everglade State College, 2018

FIGURE 2.4 Sample Chronological Résumé

e-Résumés

Your job-search portfolio is not complete until you have an electronic résumé (e-résumé). For example, some companies screen applicants as a first step by having them submit an e-résumé.

Customize Your e-Résumé for a Bot

While you will customize your résumé for each potential position, you need to understand that the first step in the hiring process could be passing the "bot test." Review the job description carefully and build into your résumé terms used in the job description.

Place a *keyword summary,* consisting of 20 to 30 words at the top of the page, after your name and contact information:

- Highlight your education, experience, and accomplishments.
- Customize your keyword summary with words taken directly from the job title and description.
- Use common industry terms to describe your skills and experience.

For an online application, send your electronic résumé attached to an email, or post it on the internet on a personal web page.

While on a traditional résumé, you will describe your work experience in verb phrases that begin with strong action verbs (such as "managed," "supervised," or "processed"), on an e-résumé, keyword summaries consist of *noun and adjective phrases,* such as "fluent in Spanish," "team-oriented," or "strong communication skills." Emphasize your knowledge, experience, and skills that are likely to attract prospective employers.

Electronic Formatting

- Use a sans-serif font, such as Arial, Calibri, or Helvetica, size 11 or 12 point.
- Use a maximum of 65 characters per line.
- Omit any kind of graphics, shading, italics, and underlines.
- Use all caps for headings.
- Do not use bullet points.

- Align left; do not justify right margins—leave the right margin uneven.
- Include a keyword summary at the top of the page, and use key words throughout, using noun and adjective phrases (rather than verbs)
- Adhere to parallel structure and end verbs in their -ing form (e.g., "answering phone and email messages").

Though traditional résumés contain tabs and bolding for headers, such as "Education" and "Experience," e-résumés lack tabs and highlighting. Here's how to change your traditional résumé into an electronic one:

1. Remove all highlighting, bolding, underlining, and italics.
2. Eliminate bullets, and replace them with dashes, small letter *o*s, or asterisks.
3. Move all your text to the left.
4. Remove hard returns, except for those separating major sections.
5. Use all caps for headers.
6. Provide an additional line of spacing between sections.
7. Save the file in ASCII or rich-text format.

To send your electronic résumé, start with a *subject line* that states the title of the job for which you are applying, such as "Research Assistant." Then, copy and paste your cover letter followed by your résumé within an email. Employers are reluctant to open attachments from people they do not know, so check first before sending your traditionally formatted résumé as an attachment.

PAT VINCENT
109 Hillcrest Avenue
Downers Grove, IL 60615
Email: pv@email.com
630-555-1212

CASE MANAGER WITH 5+ YEARS OF EXPERIENCE

KEYWORDS

Direct youth services, client-focused, collaborative, diverse computer skills, multi-disciplinary team member, youth and senior advocate for community services, high caseload ability, leadership, communication and writing skills, college graduate

OBJECTIVE

A position in which I can use my case management, communication, and leadership skills to grow within a social service organization that has a client focus.

EDUCATION

MSW, Best University

BSW, Ivy College

Related courses: social policy, research, group practice, communities and societies

Diploma, South Side High School, Downers Grove, Illinois
Graduated 2006

WORK EXPERIENCE

Case Manager, Department of Child Services, Chicago, Illinois, 2018 to present

Facilitating life skills group, maintaining a caseload of 20 families, creating behavior management plans, creating goals and objectives with clients, transporting clients to public aid appointments, recording daily and weekly case notes, providing crisis management to clients.

SKILLS

Word, Excel, PowerPoint, WordPerfect, Lotus Notes, Calendar Creator Plus, Outlook (email), Internet (Orbitz and Expedia)

FIGURE 2.5 Sample e-Résumé

Résumés vs. Curricula Vitae

In the U.S., job seekers use *résumés* to highlight their experiences and skills in a competitive job market. As discussed, résumés are one to two pages long, use strong action words, and are best tailored for each specific position, including only the most relevant background information. Though résumé styles vary, most people in the United States would agree that the résumé is a tool used to "sell yourself" to your potential employer.

In contrast, a curriculum vitae (CV) is used in the international market as well as for academic, scientific, and research positions. A CV is a history of professional and academic credentials and is less a marketing tool than a chronological record of where you have worked. The CV starts with your most-recent position, what you have studied, publications you have authored, awards you have earned, and so on. In cultures valuing context, a midcareer professional's CV might run on for many pages. In some parts of the world, CVs include photographs, marital status, age, and number of children; these attributes are considered important qualifying and "contextual" information. On the other hand, American managers expect high-impact, concise, bullet-pointed résumés and can misconstrue CVs as being long-winded and bland. For example, some international professionals respectfully understate credentials so that (high-context) readers can infer a candidate's desirability based on prestigious schools and industry stature; this approach is ineffective with low-context Americans.

In your own career, the best practice when determining whether to use a résumé or CV dictates that you get to know your audience and then rely on the *platinum rule* (treat others as *they* want to be treated). When applying for a position at an international company, gain insight into your audience by asking cultural informants about its norms and protocols for hiring and documenting performance. If possible, review documents from candidates who have been successful in the organization you are approaching.

Quick Introductory Pitch

By developing a quick introduction pitching your skills, you will be ready for any networking event or even the impromptu meeting of a potential employer. Think of the quick introduction as an elevator speech—a short monologue that provides vital information, keeping the listeners' attention and garnering their interest. Create an actual script that you memorize, but be sure to sound natural when you use it.

Here is an example of a quick introductory pitch:

> Hi. My name is Rose Lindsey, and I have a bachelor's degree in social work. As well as having extensive experience working with the elderly and disabled, I am a supportive team player with strong leadership qualities. Would you be interested in receiving my résumé, or do you have any positions that I might apply for?

Your elevator speech should take no more than 30 to 60 seconds. Give the listener enough honest information that highlights key reasons you could contribute to their company. Before you finish your conversation, get contact information and find out how you should send your information (i.e., via an electronic copy or a hard copy).

Coaching Tip

Voicemail Messages

Have you ever received a rambling voicemail message? Have you ever left one? For best results, plan your message before you call.

Here are some guidelines for leaving voice mail messages:

1. Map out the message before you call.
2. Start your message by slowly stating your name and phone number.

3. State the purpose of your call; give the most important details first.
4. Include a time frame. When do you need the information you are requesting?
5. Make sure you include the best times you can be reached.
6. Repeat your phone number slowly at the end of the message.

Writing Workshop

A. Create a Personal Letterhead

A letterhead is placed at the top of the page and contains your name and contact information, which you can use for your job-search documents, including your résumé and follow-up letters. (See examples on documents illustrated for résumés and letters.)

B. Write a Cover Letter

Write a cover letter that you could use in a job search. Use Times New Roman, size 12 font. At the paragraph tab, set controls at single spacing and 0 for "Before" and "After."

As you format your letter, consider the following:

- Did you break your letter into a short intro, body, and conclusion?
- Did you use a colon after the salutation?
- Did you use "Sincerely," as the closing?
- Did you include an enclosure notation for your résumé?

C. Write a Thank-You Message

Thank-you messages are important job-search tools. By taking the time to send a thank-you note, you set yourself apart from the crowd.

Who would you like to recognize for assisting you? A networking contact? An interviewer? A professor? A friend or family member? Write a thank-you message and send it, if you wish.

D. Write Your Hard-Copy and e-Résumés

Start the process by determining if you will use a chronological or functional format. Use the letterhead that you created in Part A of this writing workshop.

Job-Search Checklist

____ Write your career objective and purpose statement.

____ Create a personal business card.

____ Collect samples of your written work.

____ Compose a sample cover letter.

____ Prepare your résumés: chronological format and electronic format.

____ Ask two to three contacts for a letter of reference.

____ Prepare a list of networking opportunities.

____ Buy heavy-weight bond paper and envelopes for résumés and letters.

Résumé Worksheet

Job Title/Job Description

___

___

Headline

___

Career Focus/Summary

___

___

Skills/Qualities/Keyword Summary

___

Education

School/College ___ Degree to Be Conferred ___

Major: ___ Minor: ___

___

___

Work Experience

For each position, list several job duties or tasks that you performed. Start each with a strong verb and maintain parallel structure.

Position ______________________ Job Duties or Tasks ______________________

From ______ to ______ ______________________

____

Total time: ____________ ______________________

Position ______________________ Job Duties or Tasks ______________________

From ______ to ______ ______________________

____

Total time: ____________ ______________________

Position ______________________ Job Duties or Tasks ______________________

From ______ to ______ ______________________

____

Total time: ____________ ______________________

Clubs and Extracurricular Activities

____

____

JULIANNA JANULEWICZ

Oak Lawn, Illinois • 708.555.5555 • JULIANNA.JANULEWICZ@EMAIL.COM
https://www.linkedin.com/silvia.janulewica-555555

SOCIAL WORK PROFESSIONAL

Self-starter with strong communication and problem-solving skills. Team player and tactful communicator across all levels. Able to manage multiple projects and achieve excellent outcomes. Effective organizer who accomplishes tight deadlines without compromising quality. Demonstrated ability to learn rapidly, manage difficult circumstances, and adapt quickly to changing situations.

WORK EXPERIENCE

Case Worker

Shelter House, Inc., Hillside, Illinois June 2020 – Present

- Create and implement new programs for at-risk youth and addiction recovery.
- Conduct assessments and develop individualized service plans.
- Provide advocacy and support; investigate allegations of abuse and submit reports.
- Answer client calls, schedule supervised visits, and process payments.
- Manage and create content for agency media pages and other publications.
- Organize yearly symposium.

PRACTICUM/INTERNSHIP EXPERIENCE

Human Services Intern

Community Recovery Program, Orland Park, Illinois January 2020 – May 2020

- Created extensive list of addiction treatment locations in Illinois, soliciting various agencies
- Scanned and shredded confidential documents and assembled new participant packages
- Updated call log activity into database system

EDUCATION

MSW, Loyola University, Chicago
Degree to be conferred 2026

BSW, University of Illinois, Chicago Campus
May 2020

AAS, Human Services
Moraine Valley Community College
Magna Cum Laude, June 2018

SKILLS

Microsoft Office Suite – Outlook, Word, Excel, PowerPoint, Publisher | Microsoft Team | Adobe | iProcurement

JULIANNA JANULEWICZ

Oak Lawn, Illinois • 708.555.5555 • JULIANNA.JANULEWICZ@EMAIL.COM
https://www.linkedin.com/silvia.janulewica-555555

September 4, 2025

Mr. Robert L. Lindsey
Recruitment Manager
Social Work Agencies, Inc.
180 North LaSalle
Chicago, IL 60611

Dear Mr. Lindsey:

I am writing to apply for the position of program director advertised on SkillBuilder.com. My experience as a case worker in a nonprofit organization combined with my educational background in social work creates a strong foundation to build your program. My MSW degree is expected to be conferred in May 2026.

Here are my key accomplishments:

- Created and facilitated programs in addiction recovery.
- Created new programming to engage youth in emergency homeless shelters.

With a supportive style, I am adept at building relationships, consensus, and a shared sense of purpose. My skills and professional experience will meet your agency's expectations, and I'd appreciate the opportunity to bring my leadership skills and passion for helping others to your team.

I welcome a meeting to explore this opportunity and will contact you within the next week; my rèsumè is enclosed. In the meantime, feel free to contact me by email or phone. I look forward to hearing from you.

Sincerely,

Julianna Janulewicz, BSW
Résumé Enclosed

PART 3

The Interview

Everything you've done until now—your résumé, cover letter, and networking—is for the sole purpose of getting in front of a hiring manager. Now, you must be ready for the most important step in finding a job: *the interview.*

The Interview

First Impressions

People make a multitude of decisions about a person within the first few seconds of meeting. First impressions are lasting impressions, and the first thing anyone notices about you is your appearance. Thus, even for video interviews, dress appropriately (and conservatively) for the position for which you are applying. Interviewers complain that job applicants show up in T-shirts, unkempt hair, and wrinkled clothing; in addition, the interview is not the time to flaunt body art or piercings.

Know the proper etiquette; prospective employers interpret anything less as disrespectful for the organization and the position. After you have been hired, dress according to the company dress code. Everyone flourishes in conservative business attire. Though you want to express your personality, you want your prospective employer to remember you for your smile, not extreme wardrobe decisions.

Be Prompt

Being prompt means arriving *before* your scheduled appointment. Never show up late for an interview; the interviewer will interpret late behavior as an indication of your potential work habits.

If you arrive way too early, such as an hour before your scheduled appointment, drive or walk around the block a time or two. As you do, reflect on the points you will make in the interview.

Preparing for a Video Interview

1. Select a place that is quiet, free of distractions, and has a professional background. (If needed, go to your college library.)
2. Collect all materials that you might need, including a copy of your résumé (which your interviewer would also have) along with a pen and notepad.
3. Be prepared with about three questions to ask your interviewer.
4. Become familiar with the interview platform that will be used and practice using it; some top platforms include Willo, Spark Hire, myInterview, and VidCruiter.
5. Be seated and ready for the interview a few minutes early so that you can check in at the exact time the interview is scheduled to begin.
6. Dress professionally, erring on the side of dressing conservatively.
7. Remember to smile, and don't fidget.
8. Before the interview starts, take a few deep breaths. (The 4-7-8 breathing technique can be calming; breath in to the count of 4, hold for 7, and release slowly to the count of 8.)

Be Prepared

An important part of your interview is the interpersonal communication you establish with the interviewer. One way to achieve a good rapport is going to the interview prepared. Know about the company, the position, and the industry; have two or three key questions you can ask the interviewer. The interviewer will know that you have done your research on the organization by the questions you ask. For on-site interviews, greet the interviewer with a warm smile and firm, but not bone-crushing, handshake. Exhibit a positive and enthusiastic demeanor.

Whether on site or online, be aware of your body language, as your nonverbal messages can shout volumes about you. Nervous habits (such as nail biting, hair twirling, extreme hand movements, or rocking in your chair) are distractions and signal insecurity. Make good eye contact; looking away during key questions could signal to an interviewer that your answer is not honest.

When you become skillful at interviewing, you will work the discussion toward the organization's needs (the driving force for the interview) rather than focus on your own needs: "Ask not what the company can do for you ... let them know you can do for the company." Apply your listening skills so that you read the interviewer's nonverbal messages. If the interviewer stares at the clock or glances at it often, this could indicate that you are talking too much and not staying on track with the interview. Active listening will help you develop flow with the interviewer.

Demonstrate how your skills and experience counteract any issues or concerns the interviewer may express:

Interviewer's statement:	I'm concerned that you don't have enough experience for this position.
Your response:	Though I may be short on formal experience, I am a very quick learner and enjoy all of the tasks this job entails.

Be prepared with at least three questions about the position (but not yet about salary or benefits) that you can ask during or after the interview. The following questions are some appropriate examples:

- Can you tell me more about the team I will be working with?
- What will a typical day look like?
- What immediate projects are pending?
- What is your vision for the company?

At the end of the interview, just before you leave, you can get an idea of how you did by asking the following question: Do my skills and qualifications match what you are looking for? This question will give you one last chance to overcome concerns and sell your skills before the interview ends. Do not bring up salary; the topic will come up when you are made a job offer. Also, do not try to take control of the interview; leave the interviewer in charge!

The Traditional Interview

Put what you learned in developing your job-search profile to use in answering these traditional interview questions. Work alone or with a partner. As you answer these questions, give examples that demonstrate your abilities; your examples do not need to be job related. If a question doesn't apply, you may skip it; however, keep in mind that you may be asked any or all of these questions on a job interview.

Interview Questions

Tell me about yourself.

Describe your ability to solve problems.

Are you a team player? Give me some examples of how you work on a team.

How have you demonstrated leadership?

Are you an independent self-starter?

What special talents or gifts do you have? (Consider sports, music, and hobbies.) Tell me about your communication skills.

Are you a good listener? Tell me about your listening skills.

How are your writing skills? What kinds of documents do you feel confident writing?

How are your presentation skills? Do you feel comfortable presenting to a group or facilitating a meeting? (Provide examples.)

What is stronger, your people skills or technical skills? Why?

How are your computer skills? What software packages do you know well?

Do you have skill in global communications or foreign languages? (Provide examples that demonstrate your ability.)

Can you negotiate?

How about managing? ... Have you ever supervised or directed others in completing tasks?

What are your people skills like? Do you enjoy working with people? Are you easy to get along with?

Do you take responsibility for your actions?

How do you handle mistakes—your own and others'?

Do you take responsibility for your decisions when things don't turn out as planned?

If I were to ask your best friend to describe you, what would they say?

What are your weaknesses or growing edges?

Often, a person's attitude helps secure a position and contributes to promotions throughout a career. Thus, you may feel uncomfortable answering some questions, especially about mistakes or growing edges (weaknesses). However, your honest and positive approach will demonstrate that you are not defensive but, instead, have a good, realistic way of thinking.

Even when a question sounds as if it has a "yes" or "no" answer, embellish your response with examples that demonstrate your answer. Interviewers feel most comfortable in a communication exchange; they often find it difficult to be in a situation in which the applicant either speaks too little or too much. Balance is key.

The Behavioral Interview

Though preparing for the traditional interview is a good start for a job search, it isn't a final answer. Many companies apply sophisticated approaches to finding out about candidates. The behavioral interview provides the depth and sophistication companies need to predict behavior more successfully.

Behavioral interview questions probe into a person's ability to think critically, work well in teams, or reveal self-perceptions, among other qualities. These answers are found by placing an applicant in context and then asking about specific information about experiences. The various scenarios necessitate the applicant placing the experience in a broader context and giving more intricate detail about the experience. One piece of the puzzle connects to another, and the interviewer has better insight into an applicant's likely behavior. For example, here are a few behavioral interview questions:

- Tell me about a specific situation when you had to work with someone you didn't like or who didn't like you.
- Tell me about a time when you rushed to meet a deadline and had other priorities to manage at the same time.
- Give me an example when you used your problem-solving skills to make a difficult decision.
- Describe a situation in which you needed to use your leadership skills.
- Tell me about an experience dealing with an upset customer or colleague.
- Tell me how you deal with conflict and give a specific example.
- Give me an example of using your persuasive communication skills to convince someone to do something your way.

Since it is difficult to predict the questions an interviewer will ask in a behavioral interview, preparing is a challenge.

One way to handle a behavioral interview question is to use the *STAR technique* (National Careers Service, n.d.), breaking the answer into the following sections:

1. *situation*—the situation you had to deal with
2. *task*—the task you were given to do
3. *action*—the action you took
4. *result*—the result of your action and what you learned

As you apply the STAR technique, think of yourself as telling a concise, highly focused story around the event.

Obviously, an interviewer is more interested in negative events than positive ones. Search your background for difficult situations you were able to turn around or achieve positive outcomes; equip yourself with a few specific examples that you can apply to several different questions. Select examples that show strong character traits.

The traditional interview and the behavioral interview are not mutually exclusive; as you prepare for one type of interview, you also make progress with the other. The more you prepare, the better you will do (as long as you do not have rehearsed answers). You can find more information about behavioral interviews either by doing an online search or picking up a book specifically about interviewing.

Salary Requirements

Most prospective employers prefer that they initiate the issue of salary. Thus, realize that the topic will come up eventually—they know that you do not expect to work for free. Also realize that how you handle this question gives a strong impression about your goals and character. Are you solely interested in working for the highest salary you can get. or are other issues (e.g., potential to learn and develop versatile skills) just as important to you as salary?

In addition to *not* asking about salary too soon, also avoid asking about any of the following too quickly:

- How long it will take to get promoted?
- What benefits do you offer?
- How much vacation time will I get?

These types of questions can lead employers to think that you really aren't interested in the job for which you are applying. They may think that you overestimate your value and will become bored easily. If you do ask about salary directly, ask about the salary range, rather than the exact salary.

At some point, a company will either request your salary history or ask your salary requirements. Supply this information when it is requested. If you are in doubt, state that your salary requirement is flexible. However, if salary data is required as you submit your résumé, list your last salary along with a statement that "salary is negotiable based upon the right opportunity."

Interview Follow Up

After an interview, focus on two types of follow up:

1. Thank the interviewer for meeting with you. As discussed in Part 2, for every interview, send a thank-you letter, note, or message within the first day or two following your meeting.
2. Reflect on your interviewing skills to make them stronger for your next opportunity.

After the interview, develop a follow-up strategy that relates to reflection and self-growth. Evaluate how you think you did in the interview process and how you can do even better next time. What questions do you wish you had asked? What pertinent information did you leave out? What was the most positive or negative thing that occurred in the interview?

The bottom line is that the more you interview, the better you are able to hone your interview skills. As the old adage goes, *practice makes perfect*. After an interview, you may feel exhausted and are likely to hone into everything that you did "wrong." However, do not beat yourself up over what you *should* have done; now is the time to look optimistically to the future.

Job Offers

Getting a job offer is always exciting, even if you do not accept the position. Employers often make job offers through a telephone call, but an offer may also be made via email. If salary has not already been discussed, this is the perfect time to ask about salary and benefits. If the salary sounds low, ask if it is negotiable.

Accepting a Job Offer

You do not need to accept on the spot, but you should give a definite time frame in which you will convey your answer. Sound positive—even enthusiastic. You don't want your prospective employer to have doubts about you at this stage of the process. Thus, take a day or two to think about the offer and give a response. (However, before you give the employer a time frame, ask how much time you can have to consider the offer before giving your response.)

If you are positive that you want the position, it is perfectly all right to accept during the same phone call in which the position is offered. Be excited about the offer. Also realize that they are excited about you—otherwise, they wouldn't have offered you the position! Savor the moment. It won't be long before your first day on the job and you have a new set of challenges (exciting ones, though).

Resigning From the Old Job

When you resign from a company, do your best to give 2 or more weeks' notice. Your company may ask you to put your resignation in writing. In your resignation letter, don't include reasons or excuses; simply state that you are resigning, and give the effective date. However, you should be prepared to leave sooner than your resignation date, as many companies let people go as soon as they receive their resignation. On the other hand, many companies count on your giving them enough time to fill the position. By acting as a true professional, you will have fewer regrets and will retain a better reputation.

Rejecting a Job Offer

If you are offered a position that you choose not to accept, start by thanking the representative for making the offer. Then, be honest yet tactful and professional as you decline their offer. You do not need to say whether you accepted another position or why but may offer that information, if you choose.

Writing Workshop

Mock Interviews

Instructions: Do a mock interview with a partner. Have fun with this exercise, as you get valuable practice preparing for a job interview.

1. Compile a list of five questions you might be asked on an interview.
2. Compile a list of three questions that you could ask the interviewer.
3. Give your partner your list of interview questions; as your partner asks each question, give interview-quality answers.
4. After you have answered your five interview questions, ask your partner the questions you developed for the interviewer.
5. Switch roles, and repeat the interview.

PART 4

Leadership, Core Values, and Purpose

Finding a job in social work is just the beginning of what will be a long and fruitful career helping others, perhaps even saving lives in the process. By examining your leadership quality, core values, and purpose, you can go beyond developing a career portfolio by starting your "life portfolio." In fact, at some time in your life, you may decide to work on your memoirs. The work you do with these topics can feed into that kind of life project.

The Leader in You

An important element of all positions is leadership. In fact, questions about your leadership abilities and experience may come up during the interview. Even if you have never held a position of authority, you have your own unique leadership abilities and experiences, and it's important to be able to verbalize those qualities.

To develop your own leadership qualities more fully, do some self-reflective work:

- Understand your purpose.
- Identify your values, strengths, and limitations.
- Take actions that are consistent with your values.

Becoming an effective leader is a life-long process; you build your leadership skills from the way you think and the actions you take. The remainder of this section assists in identifying some of your current leadership qualities.

Your Leadership Qualities

A person doesn't wake up one day to find that they are a strong leader. Leadership skills develop over a lifetime. In many situations every day, you have opportunities to exercise your leadership skills.

What leadership qualities do you express? Consider formal and informal experiences at school, at your place of worship, in part- and full-time jobs, in group sports, and in associations and volunteer groups. The following are some words and phrases that describe qualities of strong leaders; go through the list slowly, and take note of your impressions as well as the specific experiences that come to mind:

Risk Taker / Ambitious / Good Listener / Excellent Communicator / Problem-Solver / Confident

Pushes Through Fear / Brings Out the Best in Others / Focused / Energized / Motivator / Passionate

Clearheaded / Sees the Big Picture / Thinks Outside the Box / Tries New Ideas

Gives Credit Where Credit Is Due / Gives Honest Feedback / Collaborative / Shares Responsibility

Takes Responsibility / Admits Mistakes / Committed / Dedicated / Open Minded / Visionary

Communicates the Mission / Deals With Root Causes Not Just Symptoms / Optimistic / Energizes

Mobilizes Team Toward Achieving Goals / Understands Consequences (Immediate and Long-Term)

Expresses Initiative / Self-Starter / Embraces Diversity / Team Player / Cooperative / Decisive

Entrepreneurial / Strong / Courageous / Brave / Calm Under Pressure

Here are examples of leadership qualities along with specific experiences to illustrate them:

- *mobilizes a team toward achieving a goal*—My high school basketball team was at the end of the season with no chance of winning the conference. It would have been easy to give up, but I played as strong and tough at the end of the season as I did at the beginning. As a result, my teammates played harder too, and surprisingly, we won a game against the state champions.
- *entrepreneurial*—I work as a hair stylist part-time, and I have developed a clientele. Even though I am away at school, I maintain contact with several clients and do work for them when I am home for school breaks. Some clients like my work so much that they say they would travel 50 miles just for me to cut their hair.

First, identify three leadership qualities listed above that describe you. For each quality, recall an experience in which you used your leadership skills successfully. Summarize each in the following spaces.

Leadership Qualities:

1. ______________________________
2. ______________________________
3. ______________________________

Your Peak Leadership Experiences

Think about your peak leadership experiences—situations in which you acted with integrity to influence another person or group. Include anything from grade school to the present. Describe one of these experiences in the following spaces, and explain what it was about the experience that drew upon your leadership abilities. What did you learn about yourself as a leader?

____

____

Here are other questions to provoke your thinking:

- Describe a time when a group depended on you to get a specific job done.
- Describe a time when you were in a group and a "wrong" decision was being made. How did you handle it?

Your Core Values

Your core values have already played a strong role in your career choice. Gaining additional insight into your core values will aid you in making decisions throughout your career and life.

Frederic M. Hudson and Pamela D. McLean (1995) discovered, after studying hundreds of biographies of successful adults, that people evaluated their lives based on some combination of six core values:

- *personal mastery*—to know thyself (self-esteem, confidence, identity, inner motivation, a positive sense of self, courage, sense of being a distinct person)
- *achievement*—to reach your goals (working, winning, playing in organized sports, getting results and recognition, being purposeful, focusing on "doing")
- *intimacy*—to love and be loved (bonding, caring, making relationships work, feeling close, being a friend, being connected)
- *play and creativity*—to follow your intuition (being imaginative, spontaneous, original, expressive, artistic, funny, curious, childlike, not being purposeful)
- *search for meaning*—to find wholeness (spiritual integrity, unity, integrity, peace, an inner connection to all things, spirituality, trust in the flow of life, inner wisdom, connecting with nature, connecting with a higher power, focus on being)
- *compassion and contribution*—to leave a legacy (improving, helping, feeding, reforming, leaving the world a better place, serving, social and environmental caring, institution-building, volunteering, engaging in activism)

What core value is most important to you? That's your key source of energy and passion. By focusing your energy on activities that are congruent with your most important values, you find more energy and satisfaction. In turn, when you focus on activities that are incongruent with your values, your energy and passion are sapped. In the following exercise, you make the difficult choices necessary to prioritize your core values.

A. Rank order Hudson and McLean's previously listed core values to identify which are most important to you at this point in your life (1 = most important; 6 = least important). Also write a few comments to describe how you express each value, as in the following example:

Personal Mastery: Right now, my most important goal is doing things to build my confidence so that I get a good job that leads to a great career. Every day, I try to learn more about who I really am compared to what people expect from me.

Core Values:

1. ______________________________
2. ______________________________
3. ______________________________
4. ______________________________
5. ______________________________
6. ______________________________

B. After you have ranked your core values, reflect on how you spend your time now and any changes you may make to prioritize what is important to you. For example, compare how much time and energy you are devoting to each core value with how you rank it.

Hudson and McLean also found that as people grow and change, the order of priority of these core values tends to change as well. Thus, what was a priority at age 20 may not be as important at 40 or 70.

What Is Your Purpose?

Today, most organizations have a *mission statement* that guides their decisions. A mission statement brings focus and cohesion to a company; a *purpose statement* can do the same thing for an individual.

Let's explore *purpose* and how to use it for guidance when making personal and professional choices. For example, many successful professionals in their forties and fifties wake up one day to discover that they feel unfulfilled in a career to which they have dedicated their lives. By getting in touch with purpose early on, you help ensure that your career objectives will intertwine with your life objectives—and each will enhance the other. As you deepen your understanding of purpose, you will apply it more fully to your career and life.

Purpose answers the deep questions of life:

- Who am I?
- Why am I here?
- What am I meant to do?
- How do I lead a meaningful life?

While these questions are not easy, you may find that they tug at you until you answer them; that's because humans are purpose-seeking beings. While some of us might imagine that these questions were developed in recent times, ancient tribal rituals of indigenous peoples indicate that the search for purpose has been with us for centuries. Understanding purpose has been on the hearts of humans throughout recorded history.

Twentieth-century mythologist Joseph Campbell (1988) discovered an uncanny similarity among unrelated native tribes from different parts of the world. These unrelated tribes told similar stories of how they sent young adults on a quest for meaning to find their own purpose. As a rite of passage to adulthood, a child would leave the tribe on a journey in quest of uncovering their purpose. The newly christened adult would return to the tribe, ready to live purposefully within the local community.

Lacking these ancient rituals, many of us overlook the process of uncovering our own life purpose. As you explore your own purpose, as presented here, complete the included reflection exercises so that your purpose statement can guide your work choices.

Purpose Is Unique

At one point or another, most people doubt the unique qualities of their lives. A starting point in finding your purpose is realizing that no one can offer exactly what you can to the world, in quite the way that you can do it. No one else has the same set of gifts, values, life experiences, and passionate concerns that you possess. As a result, your purpose is uniquely yours and different from everyone else's.

After reflecting on your gifts, values, life experiences and passionate concerns, you will come to realize that it is not even possible for another human to be the same as you are. In a world filled with billions of people, you and your purpose are unique.

Purpose Is Uncovered, Not Discovered

As you write your purpose statement, don't look for something outside of yourself that sounds impressive but that has little to do with the real you. Don't be concerned about writing something that sounds good to others, but instead, focus on writing a statement that really describes you.

Purpose is uncovered by looking inward, engaging in a process of self-reflection. You are not finding something new; it's a matter of uncovering what is already within you. Raising your own awareness of what feels fulfilling and gives your life meaning isn't easy. Self-reflection is challenging because it requires quiet—real silence. Most of us find it difficult to focus on *feeling* and *being* instead of the *thinking* and *doing* that typically dominate our lives. Real quiet can be a particular challenge if you have integrated technology into your way of living. Most of us crave constant stimulation, and technology-driven interruptions are part of life. When everything is turned off, the real quiet that results can feel overwhelming. Technology has become so ingrained in our lives that we may have a hard time separating from it when we finally take the time to reflect. People work on tablets and laptops while "reflecting" in nature preserves and even answer text messages while attending religious services. Experiencing real quiet means making your life a high priority; you must be willing to shut everything off to open the space needed to explore your purpose.

Purpose Evolves Over Time

Regardless of your current age, your purpose will continue to evolve over time. It is not too early for a 10-year-old to consider purpose, nor is it too late for a person approaching 90. Some people have a clear sense of direction right away; others are in the fog for years before clarity comes. Start from where you are, and reflect on the question of purpose, raising your consciousness of it in all aspects of your life. Your sense of purpose will evolve and deepen if you are willing to commit to working on it over the long term. Purpose is a series of continual adjustments over the journey of a lifetime.

Purpose Guides Work Choices

The word "purpose" comes from the Latin word "proponere," which means "to put forward." When you are clear about your purpose, you are putting forward your intention to live your life in a particular way.

Being intentional means making choices. Consciously consider all possibilities and make deliberate choices instead of letting possibilities choose your direction. Making a choice is powerful because choosing one direction means excluding another.

Sometimes, people don't want to make a choice because they want to keep their freedom and their options open. However, the opposite is also true: trying to live with all possible options can be a heavy load to bear. Full commitment to a conscious decision can feel liberating. Narrowing possibilities is a source of freedom, so commit to your purpose and lighten your load.

After you settle on the type of work that represents the best expression of your purpose, your next choice is whether to join an organization or work independently by forming your own company. If your purpose and your company's purpose are aligned, it increases the possibility that you will be able to express your purpose at work.

Practice

Writing a Purpose Statement

Instructions: Write a two- to three-sentence purpose statement. The first step in writing your purpose statement is looking for themes about your passionate concerns, deep interests, and natural talents. Make notes about what you notice, and follow these steps:

1. Write several different drafts of a purpose statement. Begin each sentence with "My purpose is to ..." (an action verb will follow, such as "my purpose is to design ..."). Simply let the words flow, and do not be concerned about writing coherent sentences. You will have an opportunity to edit later.
2. Over the period of a few days, reread your purpose statement drafts, noticing how they feel to you. Take note of any words, phrases, or clauses that are emotionally appealing. Read the drafts out loud. Take note of any words or phrases that quicken your heart when you hear them.
3. Write a new draft of your purpose statement, incorporating the words that you emotionally connected with in step 2.
4. Read your revised draft to a partner and get feedback.

Writing Workshop

A. Writing a Self-Appraisal

Instructions: Write an honest self-appraisal, starting with the following questions:

- What are my strengths and best qualities?
- What are some recent accomplishments?
- What are my growing edges?

Next, write two or three goals, identify specific steps to achieve them, and include a time frame for each step. By including a time frame, you are creating an *action plan.*

Finally, write yourself a letter identifying your best qualities and highlighting your skills and abilities. Give yourself the same words of encouragement that you would give your best friend. Keep your letter, and refer to it periodically.

B. Writing Your Story

Instructions: To begin, write a 6- to 10-page paper on the story of your life. In particular, explore the following areas:

- Recall the earliest instance when you declared what you want to do when you grow up. Write about how your vocational declarations deepened or changed over time.
- Describe the influential people in your life and the impact they had on your life. Who are your heroes?
- Explain the major events that had a life-changing effect on you.
- Describe the natural talents that other people notice in you; go as far back as you can remember. (We all have gifts or natural talents. Since they are natural, they are often overlooked because they come easy to us.)

C. Leaving a Legacy

Instructions: Write out your responses to the following questions:

1. How old do you believe you will live to be?
2. Imagining that you are that age and looking back on your life, what do you want to be able to say about the legacy of your life?
3. What might you do with your remaining time between now and then so that when you look back on your life, you have no regrets about how you lived it?

Quick Guide to Email and Letter Formatting

Email Format

Although email standards vary somewhat, all professional writing follows standard rules for grammar, punctuation, and abbreviation. Though more casual than a business letter, an email is a business document that portrays an image of you and your company. Therefore, do not be too casual over email, and consider the following tips:

- Start an email with a *greeting*. Use the recipient's name to create a personal link, as in "Hi Margaret."
    - Since email is somewhat informal, the word "Dear" does not need to be part of the salutation.
    - However, if you do not know the recipient and your email is your first communication, use the recipient's last name preceded by "Dear" (e.g., "Dear Mr. Stevens:").
- Use an accurate *subject line*, and update it as your conversation evolves.
- Use a simple *closing*, such as "Best regards," "All the best," "Enjoy your day," or "Take care," among others.
- For professional messages, include a sign-off that lists your name, address, phone number, and other relevant contact information.
- Email is best when the message is short, about one screen in length.
    - Start with the most important information, and get right to the point.
    - If you need the reader to take action, put that information at the beginning of the message.

To ... Regina Piper
Cc ...
Subject: Community Outreach Worker

Dear Regina,

Your position for a community outreach worker interests me, matching my skills and abilities.

As you will see by my attached resume, I have a BSW from Indiana University and an MSW from Michigan State University. With two years of related experience, I am prepared to meet the challenges of the position and contribute to your team of experts.

I look forward to hearing from you about this exciting position.

Best regards,

Bobbie

Bobbie Allison, MSW
Chicago, IL 60610
Phone: 312-555-1212

FIGURE QG.1 Effective Email

Email vs. Text Messaging

A strong boundary exists between professional email messages and text messaging. *Never* use text abbreviations in professional messages. For example, *never* use "i" for the personal pronoun "I," which should *always* be capitalized. When using contractions in an email, make sure you spell them correctly by using apostrophes (e.g., "don't" and "can't," *not* "dont" and "cant"). Because your email software may not correct spelling errors, be vigilant to avoid introducing serious proofreading errors without correcting them.

Setting Paragraph Controls

When typing a business letter, start the process by setting your paragraph controls:

- At the paragraph tab, set the spacing for "Before" and "After" to 0.
- Set line spacing to single or multiple 1.2.

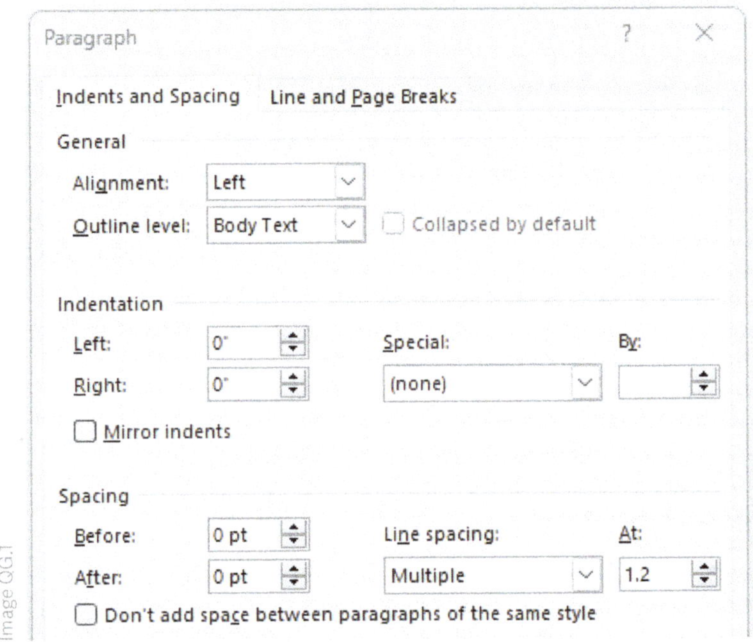

Image QG.1

Basic Parts of a Letter

1. *letterhead*—A letterhead contains information such as the name, address, phone number, fax number, and web address of a company or individual.
2. *dateline*—The dateline appears 3 lines below the letterhead (for longer letters) *or* no more than 2.5 inches from the top of the page (for shorter letters). Most software programs give a 1-inch top margin, so space down 6 to 9 lines to type the date.
3. *inside address*—The inside address contains the name (if known), title, and company name and address of the recipient. (Do not abbreviate other than using two-letter state

abbreviations, such as "IL" for Illinois.) Space down two times after typing the inside address.

4. *salutation*—The traditional greeting for letters starts with "Dear," as in "Dear Mr. Jones:" or "Dear Sue:" (follow the salutation with a *colon*, as shown). Space down two times after typing the inside address.
5. *body*—The text of your message should be single spaced; use block style (do *not* indent paragraphs). Space down two times between paragraphs and before the closing.
6. *closing*—A common closing is "Sincerely," which is followed by a comma. Space down four times after the closing before typing your name.
7. *writer's signature block*—This includes the writer's name along with a title, when used.
8. *enclosure notation*—This notation alerts the recipient (and you) that something is enclosed with the letter.

Note the following:

- If you do not have the recipient's name, use a generic title, such as "Dear Human Relations Director" or "Dear Job-Search Committee."
- Keep letters to one page in length, if possible.
- For addresses, do not abbreviate other than using the two-letter state abbreviations, such as "MI" for Michigan).
- Use the print preview function to make sure your margins have a "picture frame" effect.

Salley James, BSW
2304 North Sedgewick Avenue
Chicago, IL 60611
555-555-5555 | svjames@email.com

May 5, 2024

Mr. Robert Lindsey
Human Resource Manager
Domestic Shelter Services, Inc.
333 West Washington Street
Bolingbrook, IL 60440

Dear Mr. Lindsey:

Your position for a child and family social worker appeals to me because your requirements match my interests, skills, and experience.

As an advocate for at-risk children, I have extensive experience assisting in child welfare investigations as well as connecting families to social work services. In my position at Community Hospital, I assisted in counseling family units and staying up to date on children's wellbeing. During my internship, I supported a team of three social workers in helping to place children in foster or adoptive homes.

I will contact you the week of May 15 to explore the possibility of scheduling an interview. In the meantime, I would look forward to hearing from you.

Sincerely,

Salley James, BSW
Résumé Enclosed

FIGURE QG.2 Blocked Business Letter

Credit

IMG QG.1: Generated with Microsoft Word. Software Copyright © by Microsoft.

References

Belli, G. (2017, April 6). *How many jobs are found through networking, really? PayScale*. https://www.payscale.com/career-news/2017/04/many-jobs-found-networking

Gershon, I. (2017). *"A friend of a friend" is no longer the best way to find a job.* Harvard Business Review. https://hbr.org/2017/06/a-friend-of-a-friend-is-no-longer-the-best-way-to-find-a-job

U.S. Bureau of Labor Statistics. (n.d.). *What social workers do*. https://www.bls.gov/ooh/community-and-social-service/social-workers.htm#tab-2

National Careers Service. (n.d.). *The STAR method*. https://nationalcareers.service.gov.uk/careers-advice/interview-advice/the-star-method

Hudson, F. M., & McLean, P. D. (1995). *Life launch: A passionate guide to the rest of your life*. The Hudson Institute Press.

Campbell, J. (1988). *Joseph Campbell and the power of myth*. Mystic Fire Video.

Anderson, G. (1999). Forward. In S. Kravetz, *Girl boss: Running the show like the big chicks*. Girl Press.

Henderson, R. (2024, June 4). *How to write a resume for today's job market*. Jobscan. https://www.jobscan.co/blog/how-to-write-a-resume/

Index

www.ingramcontent.com/pod-product-compliance
Ingram Content Group UK Ltd.
Pitfield, Milton Keynes, MK11 3LW, UK
UKHW021829270726
14058UKWH00001B/57

9 798823 354530